Comedies for Kids

Comedies
for Kids

DUNCAN BALL

Illustrated by
CRAIG SMITH

ANGUS
& ROBERTSON
PUBLISHERS

For Greg

Angus & Robertson Publishers' creative writing programme is assisted by the Australia Council, the Federal Government's arts funding and advisory body.

ANGUS & ROBERTSON PUBLISHERS

Unit 4, Eden Park, 31 Waterloo Road, North Ryde, NSW, Australia 2113, and 16 Golden Square, London WIR 4BN, United Kingdom

First published in Australia by Angus & Robertson Publishers in 1988 First published in the United Kingdom by Angus & Robertson (UK) in 1988

Copyright © Duncan Ball 1988

National Library of Australia Cataloguing-in-publication data.

Ball, Duncan, 1941–
  Comedies for kids.

  ISBN 0 207 15574 7.

  1. Children's plays, Australian. I. Smith, Craig,
  1955– . I. Title.
A822'.3

Typeset in Hong Kong by Compset Production Co. Ltd.
Printed in Australia by Globe Press

CONTENTS

INTRODUCTION

This collection of short plays and skits was designed either for performance on the stage or in the classroom or simply to be read and enjoyed. They range in cast from a stand-up comedy routine for one actor to a play with twenty speaking parts plus extras. They are all chock-a-block with time-honoured humour. Or, to put it differently, they're full of corny old jokes.

Duncan Bell

CHARACTERS

Sam Shovel
Liz Dizzy

NOTE

This is an easy skit that can be done with no props or with a simple set. It can be done without costumes or with SAM SHOVEL in the 1940s detective's crumpled suit and felt hat and LIZ DIZZY in a wide-brimmed hat and tight-fitting dress. The note "Aside" just means that the character speaking says his lines aloud, but to himself, instead of to the other character. Actors often face the audience when they do this.

SCENE

The scene is a detective's office. In it are a desk with a chair behind it and another chair in front of the desk for LIZ DIZZY. There is a peeling sign on the door that says, SAM SHOVEL, PRIVATE EAR. SAM SHOVEL is sitting behind the desk as the scene opens.

THE PLAY

SHOVEL: It was raining cats and dogs when I hailed a taxi and went to my office. The sign on the door was peeling and three mice were doing a polka over yesterday's sandwich. I went in and dusted off the telephone (*He dusts the telephone with a handkerchief.*) that hadn't rung for a week. It was one of those miserable days that makes you think of elephants in ballet slippers riding bicycles and giraffes drifting around in hanggliders — or at least that's what it made me think of. I hadn't felt so bad since I was shipwrecked off the coast of Zanzibar when I was a baby and had to live on a tin of biscuits — which would have been OK but I kept falling off the tin. I put my feet on my desk (*He puts his feet on the desk.*) and was just wondering how I was going to get the six weeks rent I owed my landlady when in walks this dizzy blonde...

(*LIZ DIZZY enters.*)

LIZ: Good afternoon. I'm Liz Dizzy. Are you Sam Spade, private eye?

SHOVEL: No, I'm Sam Shovel, private ear.

(*LIZ DIZZY sits.*)

LIZ:	Private ear? I've never heard of a private ear. What's the difference between a private eye and a private ear?
SHOVEL:	The difference is: you can see a private eye but you can't hear a private ear.
LIZ:	Well that explains it then.
SHOVEL:	It does?
LIZ:	The reason I am here, Mr Shovel, is that I'd like you to unearth some information for me. That is what you do, isn't it?
SHOVEL:	Shovel's the name, digging's the game. I'll unearth the information until you have the *whole* story and then I'll fill you in. What do you want me to do?
LIZ:	There's a man I want you to find.
SHOVEL:	Nothing to it. Consider him found. How much can you pay?
LIZ:	What do you charge for finding people?
SHOVEL:	A modest sixty dollars a week — cash in advance — buys you my Super A1 Search.
LIZ:	That is modest. What do you do in a Super A1 Search?
SHOVEL:	I wait till the gentleman in question walks in here by mistake.
LIZ:	But he could be anywhere. He might be living in a tent in Turkey.
SHOVEL:	Then it could take some time. And there's no time to waste so you'd better give me sixty dollars right away.
LIZ:	Isn't there a quicker way to find him?
SHOVEL:	Well there's always the Super A1 Extra Special Search for only ninety dollars a week.
LIZ:	That sounds better. What do you do for a Super A1 Extra Special Search?
SHOVEL:	Either he walks in here by accident or he gets a wrong telephone number and rings me by mistake and before he hangs up I ask him who he is and if he's the guy in question, I've found him. Good, eh?
LIZ:	But he could be in an igloo in Alaska without any phone.
SHOVEL:	I see. Then I recommend the Super A1 Extra Special All Expenses Paid To The Ends Of The Earth Search with guaranteed results.

LIZ:	How much will that cost?
SHOVEL:	That'll be ten thousand dollars if I find him and five thousand if I don't, cash in advance.
LIZ:	Five thousand if you don't? But you said it was guaranteed.
SHOVEL:	It's guaranteed that either I'll find him or I won't. Don't be a cheapskate. Take a chance.
LIZ:	OK, Mr Shovel, you've got a deal.
SHOVEL:	Give me all the details. Start at the beginning.
LIZ:	It all started when I was a child.
SHOVEL:	What did?
LIZ:	My life.
SHOVEL:	Could we get down to the case, Mrs Dizzy.
LIZ:	Yes indeed. I'll be brief.
SHOVEL:	(*Aside.*) Oh, I see, a briefcase.
LIZ:	Many years ago I read a history of an island in the Indian Ocean.
SHOVEL:	(*Aside.*) A case history, was it?
LIZ:	No, this was a book.
SHOVEL:	(*Aside.*) Ahah! A bookcase.
LIZ:	I just had to go there so I grabbed my baby and quickly packed some bags.
SHOVEL:	(*Aside.*) Ahah! A packing case.
LIZ:	And caught the first plane to Spain. Or was it the first train to the Ukraine? Then I bought a coat.
SHOVEL:	You bought a coat?
LIZ:	I caught a boat.
SHOVEL:	I see. What kind of boat was it?
LIZ:	It was a deep-she fishing boat.
SHOVEL:	A deep-*she* fishing boat?
LIZ:	Yes. They were fishing for mermaids.
SHOVEL:	(*Aside.*) I might have guessed.

6

LIZ:	Halfway to Zanzibar we were surrounded by sharks.
SHOVEL:	Did you say, (*With special emphasis.*) Zanzibar?
LIZ:	Yes, Zanzibar. The sharks circled round and round and finally the captain reached out to hook one but it bit off his arm.
SHOVEL:	Which one?
LIZ:	I don't know, they all looked alike. Suddenly a whale came up under the boat and threw it twenty metres into the air with its enormous back fin.
SHOVEL:	(*Aside.*) Sounds like a tall tail.
LIZ:	The ship was thrown on some rocks and wrecked. It began shaking all over.
SHOVEL:	(*Aside.*) It must have been a nervous wreck.

LIZ: That all happened many years ago off the coast of Zanzibar. That's when I lost my baby. The last I saw of him he was drifting out to sea. He had to live on a tin of biscuits — (*Aside.*) which would have been OK but he kept falling off the tin.

SHOVEL: Did you say, (*With special emphasis.*) Zanzibar?

LIZ: Yes. And now I want you to find him. I'm sure he survived. Don't you see, Mr Shovel? Somewhere out there my baby is a thinking, feeling man living under a new name and wondering where his mother is.

SHOVEL: Hold on a minute. How old would your baby be now?

LIZ: About your age.

SHOVEL: What colour eyes did he have?

LIZ: The same as yours.

SHOVEL: Hair?

LIZ: He didn't have much.

SHOVEL: How tall would he be now?

LIZ: I don't know. I guess about. . .
(*She holds her hand out in front of her and he slides his head under it, and then straightens up.*)

SHOVEL: You see, I too was cast adrift off the coast of Zanzibar when I was a baby. I too had to live on a tin of biscuits — (*Aside.*) which would have been OK but I too kept falling off the tin.

LIZ: Did you say, (*With special emphasis.*) Zanzibar?
(*They give each other a meaningful look and then throw their arms around each other.*)

SHOVEL: Mum!

LIZ: Son! I've found you at last! It is you, isn't it? You are my baby, aren't you?

SHOVEL: Yes, Mother, it's me. (*He releases her.*) That'll be ten thousand dollars, please.

LIZ: Ten thousand dollars? You would charge your own mother ten thousand dollars for finding yourself when you didn't even have to look?

SHOVEL: The ten thousand is not for finding me, it's the pocket money you owe me. It'll be another ten grand for finding me.

CURTAIN

CHARACTERS

Camilla the Hun
Isaac, her servant

NOTE

This skit can also be done without props. If props are used, a couple are important: a wine bottle and at least two prop cooked fowls.

SCENE

Camilla is lying on a pile of cushions in her tent, reading a letter.

THE PLAY

CAMILLA:	(*Calling.*) Isaac, come here immediately!
	(*ISAAC runs in and bows.*)
ISAAC:	What is it, Your Highness?
CAMILLA:	I've just received this letter in the morning post. It says there's an army coming our way. They're after me, Camilla the Hun, and my lands.
ISAAC:	(*Aside.*) An attack!
CAMILLA:	That's not all. They're riding those hairy beasts with the short legs.
ISAAC:	(*Aside.*) A yak attack!
CAMILLA:	In a few minutes they'll be pulling down our tents and stealing our belongings.
ISAAC:	You mean, they'll sack and ransack. Who is their leader?
CAMILLA:	Black Jack. The madman.
ISAAC:	(*Aside.*) Black Jack the Maniac!
CAMILLA:	There's no way we can fight off his army.
ISAAC:	(*Aside.*) Alas, alack, we can't hold them back.

CAMILLA: He'll steal everything he can lay his hands on.

ISAAC: (*Aside.*) A kleptomaniac! I'd better pack!

CAMILLA: Quickly, Isaac, put all those odds and ends in that bag with the straps on it.

ISAAC: (*Aside.*) I'll put the knick-knacks and bric-a-brac in the rucksack.

CAMILLA: You're good at that.

ISAAC: (*Aside.*) I have the knack.

CAMILLA: We'll load the bag on a beast and then take the trail out of this dead end valley, paddle across the river in one of those little boats, cut our way through the ferns and then camp out in one of those big piles of hay. Not a nasty little one but one of those beautiful big ones.

(*CAMILLA gets up to go.*)

ISAAC: Let me get this straight. We'll pack the rucksack on a yak and then take the track out of the cul-de-sac and paddle the kayak and then hack through the bracken and bivouac in a crackerjack haystack. Is that it?

CAMILLA: Yes. And don't forget to bring along a little something for me to eat.

ISAAC: I'll pack you a snack.

CAMILLA: Bring me one of those cooked birds. (*Points to some cooked fowls.*)

ISAAC: The ones that go *cluck*?

CAMILLA: No, the other ones.

(*CAMILLA exits.*)

ISAAC: (*Aside.*) Ah! The ones that go *quack*! (*Grabs a fowl and puts it under him arm.*)

CAMILLA: (*From off-stage.*) And bring something to drink in case we're gone a long time.

(*ISAAC puts the bottle under his arm.*)

ISAAC: (*Aside.*) I'll bring the cognac ... because we won't be back.

(*ISAAC exits running.*)

CURTAIN

The Perils
of Prince Percy
of
Pomegranate

CHARACTERS

Prince Percy
Lord Chamberlain
Herald
Two Guards
Astrologer
Captain of the Guards
Fool
Headsman
A Mob of Peasants (*12 have speaking parts*)

STAGING

The play takes place all in one room, the throne room of a castle.
All entrances and exits are through one door. There is a window
as well. More windows, hanging banners and stonework walls
could be used for effect if desired.

COSTUMES AND PROPS

The play can be performed with few, if any, costumes and props or with full court regalia. If props are used, the most important ones are:

PRINCE PERCY's throne, crown and sceptre.
A doctor's white coat and a towel.
The FOOL's mask, preferably a half-face funny mask
with a long nose. Also a twin-coned fool's hat.
A plumed hat for the CAPTAIN OF THE GUARDS.
A hood for the HEADSMAN and a double-bladed axe
and chopping block.
A deck of cards.
Confetti.
A telescope.

For a full production a few more props could be added including a doctor's reflector and stethoscope and pitchforks for the peasants. The costumes could be the usual mock-medieval gear with tights and pointy shoes.

CHARACTERISATION

The roles can be played by either boys or girls. It might be better to have the PRINCE, the FOOL and the HEADSMAN all the same sex as they turn out to be brothers. Though in the play they are supposed to look identical, it will help the humour if they looked different.

There are two types of character in the play: the courtiers who are weak and conniving, and the peasants who are strong and conniving. Over-acting all around is the key to good performances in this play.

PRINCE PERCY is a spoiled brat, devilish when he's in control and bursting into tears when he's not.

The LORD CHAMBERLAIN is completely straight-faced and correct, as is the CAPTAIN OF THE GUARDS and the HERALD.

The ASTROLOGER is cunning and comic, as is the FOOL who is anything but a fool.

The PEASANTS should be dim-witted and dull.

<u>S</u>CENE

The throne room at Percy, Prince of Pomegranate's castle. The PRINCE is playing with a deck of cards. The HERALD comes in and holds up an imaginary horn.

THE PLAY

HERALD:	Ta da. Ta da. Ta da. Announcing the Lord Chamberlain, Your Highness.
	(*The LORD CHAMBERLAIN enters and bows. The HERALD exits.*)
CHAMBERLAIN:	Your Highness —
PRINCE:	(*Holding out the deck of cards.*) Take a card, any card.
CHAMBERLAIN:	But Your Highness —
PRINCE:	(*Fanning out the cards.*) Just take one, Lord Chambermaid.
CHAMBERLAIN:	That's Chamberlain, Your Highness, and we must have a talk.
PRINCE:	Just take a card.
	(*The LORD CHAMBERLAIN takes a card and starts to look at it.*)
PRINCE:	No, don't look at it. Now put it back in the deck.
	(*The LORD CHAMBERLAIN puts it back and the PRINCE shuffles the deck. He then looks through the cards and pulls one out and shows it to the LORD CHAMBERLAIN.*)
PRINCE:	Is this your card? (*The LORD CHAMBERLAIN looks puzzled for a minute and the PRINCE bursts into laughter.*) Isn't that a great joke? Huh? Isn't it?
CHAMBERLAIN:	Yes, Your Highness, very good, but we have important things to discuss.
PRINCE:	What could be more important than a good joke?
CHAMBERLAIN:	Well, that's quite right, Your Highness, but of course there are the affairs of state.
PRINCE:	Not the peasants again.
CHAMBERLAIN:	They're not happy with . . . well . . . with . . . the way things are.
PRINCE:	You mean *me*, Percy, Prince of Pomegranate. (*The LORD CHAMBERLAIN giggles at his name.*) I can't help my name! . . . They're not happy with me, are they Lord Chambermaid?
CHAMBERLAIN:	Chamberlain. To be frank —

PRINCE: Pleased to meet you, Frank. (*He laughs and shakes the LORD CHAMBERLAIN's hand.*)

CHAMBERLAIN: They hate your guts.

PRINCE: Oh, no! (*Burst into tears.*) They're just ungrateful, that's all. I've been so good to them. Didn't I hold a ball for them at the end of the harvest last year.

CHAMBERLAIN: That was two years ago and you charged them admission.

PRINCE: Well they didn't have to come, did they?

CHAMBERLAIN: No, not if they didn't mind having their land taken away.

PRINCE: But I needed money for the food, didn't I? And to clean the carpet after they tracked all that dirt in. Peasants are such grubs.

CHAMBERLAIN: I understand, Your Highness. But they look at things in a rather different way. They say that you charge them so much rent that everything in Pomegranate Castle belongs to *them*, carpets and all. And they say that you keep them so poor that they have to work night and day just to make enough money to live on. They say that sending the iron gate to Pomegranate Castle Bridge away to have it gold plated was unnecessary —

PRINCE: (*Screams.*) Unnecessary?! Did they say unnecessary?! Of course it's unnecessary — but it's pretty. Peasants don't understand beauty. Just wait till the gate comes back and the rays of the morning sun twinkle on every golden spike. (*Sighs.*)

CHAMBERLAIN: And they don't think it's necessary to throw wild parties for all the princes and princesses in the kingdom and give them all expensive gifts.

PRINCE: They're just jealous because they weren't born princes and princesses.

CHAMBERLAIN: That could be, Sir.

PRINCE: Why don't they throw their own party?

CHAMBERLAIN: That's what I wanted to talk about.

PRINCE: (*His eyes light up.*) They're having a party? Can I go?

CHAMBERLAIN: I wouldn't advise it, Your Highness.

PRINCE: Why not? I won't eat much.

CHAMBERLAIN: Well it's not exactly that sort of party.

PRINCE: Don't be silly. What other sort of party is there?

CHAMBERLAIN: There's The PAPPOP Party.

PRINCE: The PAPPOP Party?

CHAMBERLAIN: The PAPPOP Party. That stands for Peasants Against Prince Percy of Pomegranate. I'm afraid there's a revolt in progress.

PRINCE: You mean the peasants are revolting?

CHAMBERLAIN: Exactly, Sir.

PRINCE: (*Bursts into tears again and pounds his fists on the arms of the throne.*) I knew it! They hate me! (*Soberly.*) Could we have them all killed?

CHAMBERLAIN: They wouldn't stand for it.

PRINCE: (*Sobs.*) Then what am I to do?

CHAMBERLAIN: There's a lot of money in the treasury. I suggest you give them half their last taxes back. That might make them happy.

PRINCE: No! No! No! Never! Peasants are peasants and they're meant to suffer while monarchs have a good time. Don't they understand that?

CHAMBERLAIN: If you don't give them some money back, I think there's going to be big trouble.

PRINCE: (*Pointing to the door.*) Leave my presence at once, Lord Chambermaid —

CHAMBERLAIN: Chamberlain.

PRINCE: — I don't like your answers, they cost too much.

(*The LORD CHAMBERLAIN exits.*)

PRINCE:	Guards!
	TWO GUARDS come in.
GUARDS:	(*Together.*) Yes, Your Highness.
PRINCE:	Send in my astrologer.
GUARDS:	Your what, Sir?
PRINCE:	The bloke with the telescope.
GUARDS:	Oh, *that* astrologer. Coming right in.
	(*The TWO GUARDS step out and the HERALD comes in.*)
HERALD:	Ta da. Ta da. Ta dum dum da.
	(*The PRINCE puts a finger in his ear as if the noise has hurt it.*)
HERALD:	Announcing the court astrologer.
	(*The ASTROLOGER comes in and the HERALD goes out. The ASTROLOGER is holding a long telescope in his hand.*)
PRINCE:	My dear and faithful and trusted astrologer. How's business?
ASTROLOGER:	(*Looking out the window up at the sky with his telescope.*) Business is looking up, Your Highness.
PRINCE:	And what fortunes do the heavens hold for the Princedom of Pomegranate?
ASTROLOGER:	In the short term or the long term?
PRINCE:	In the long term.
ASTROLOGER:	Well, in the long term there isn't going to be a short term. And in the short term there may not be a short term either.
PRINCE:	You mean ... ?
ASTROLOGER:	Yes. Times are tough.
PRINCE:	Tell me more.
ASTROLOGER:	(*Looking around the sky again with the telescope.*) Well, let's see now. You were born on a Taurus Gemini cusp and at this very moment Scorpio is rising and the moon is in the seventh house ... um ... er.
PRINCE:	But what does it mean?
ASTROLOGER:	(*He is now looking straight out the window with the telescope.*) It means that a group of concerned citizens —

PRINCE:	(*Aside.*) Concerned citizens. That's the peasants!
ASTROLOGER:	— will approach a big house —
PRINCE:	(*Aside.*) Big house. That's Pomegranate Castle!
ASTROLOGER:	— to speak to a great man —
PRINCE:	(*Aside.*) Great man. That's me! And they want their money back! (*To the ASTROLOGER.*) *This is amazing! How did you predict this?*
ASTROLOGER:	Easy. (*Handing the telescope to the PRINCE.*) Have a look for yourself. They're coming this way.
PRINCE:	They are! Look at them! Now I suppose they'll want me to leave the princedom immediately. Well, I'm not going to do it! Hard cheese to them! (*He blows a raspberry.*) — to you, peasants!
ASTROLOGER:	They don't want you to go away.
PRINCE:	They don't?
ASTROLOGER:	No, then they couldn't execute you.

PRINCE: Execute me? Are you sure, O wise astrologer? How do you know they want to execute me?

ASTROLOGER: I was studying my charts down at the Bull and Thistle and having a tankard of ale last night when I noticed that Jupiter and Saturn were coming into line for the first time in two hundred years. Then I thought of your Taurus Gemini cusp and was just placing the right numbers and angles on the chart and gazing into my crystal ball when it hit me.

PRINCE: The answer?

ASTROLOGER: No, the crystal ball. It rolled off the table and hit my foot. And when I chased after it —

PRINCE: Your foot?

ASTROLOGER: No, the crystal ball. I heard something that indicated that the denizens of the Bull and Thistle were contemplating a little cranial decoupage.

PRINCE: (*Grimacing to the audience.*) They were contemplating that?

ASTROLOGER: Yes, they want to cut your head off. I'm afraid the peasants are revolting.

PRINCE: Are you sure?

ASTROLOGER: I'm almost positive. I heard one of them say: "Let's cut the prince's head off." And the rest of them cheered. (*Pointing out the window.*) If there's any doubt just look at the bloke with the black hood over his head.

PRINCE: (*Looks through the telescope.*) The one carrying the double-bladed axe?

ASTROLOGER: That's the one.

PRINCE: (*Bursts into tears again.*) Oh woe, woe, woe. Cut my head off? Oh no, no, no. (*The ASTROLOGER nods "yes, yes, yes" as the PRINCE says "no, no, no."*)

ASTROLOGER: Will that be all, Sir?

PRINCE: Yes, you may go.

ASTROLOGER: (*Grabbing the telescope from the PRINCE and hurrying towards the door.*) (*Aside.*) Good, I've got some packing to do.

PRINCE: Guards!

(*The TWO GUARDS come in.*)

GUARDS: (*Together.*) Yes, Your Highness.

PRINCE: Get me the Captain of the Guards.

GUARDS: The what, Your Highness?

PRINCE: The bloke with the feather in his hat.

GUARDS: Oh, *that* Captain of the Guards, Sir.

(*The GUARDS go out and the HERALD comes in and holds the imaginary horn in the air.*)

HERALD: Ta da. Ta da. Ta diddly-dum ta da. Announcing the Captain of the Guards.

(*The HERALD goes out as the CAPTAIN comes in.*)

PRINCE:	Barricade the castle and prepare for a siege. The peasants are revolting. (*To the audience.*) It's amazing how many times you can get away with that line.
CAPTAIN:	It's no good, Your Highness.
PRINCE:	Well they keep laughing at it —
CAPTAIN:	Not your funny line, Sir. I mean it's no good trying to barricade the castle. It can't be defended any longer.
PRINCE:	Why not? What idiot has ruined our defences? Who is he? I'll have him flogged. Send for the torturer.
CAPTAIN:	The idiot who sent the main gate off to be gold plated.
PRINCE:	Cancel the torturer. Now what can we do?
CAPTAIN:	There's no way to keep the peasants out. They'll come straight over the bridge that used to have the gate on it and across the moat.
PRINCE:	The army will hold them off.
CAPTAIN:	They've gone on holidays.
PRINCE:	Since when?
CAPTAIN:	Since they saw the peasants coming a few minutes ago.
PRINCE:	Then what will we do?
CAPTAIN:	I suggest we *all* go on holidays — fast.
PRINCE:	(*Looking out the window.*) It's too late. They'll be coming to the bridge soon, the one that used to have the gate on it. And that's the only way out of the castle. (*Aside.*) Why did I send the gate off to be gold plated?
CAPTAIN:	May I go now?
PRINCE:	Yes. It's hopeless. I may as well call in my fool.
CAPTAIN:	(*Hurrying towards the door.*) Good, I have some packing to do. (*To the audience.*) I think I know a way out the back.
PRINCE:	Guards!
	(*The TWO GUARDS enter.*)
GUARDS:	(*Together.*) Yes, Your Highness.
PRINCE:	Send in my fool.
GUARDS:	Your what, Sir?

PRINCE: He's got a funny mask with a long nose and ice cream cones on his head.

GUARDS: (*Slowly and deliberately.*) Ice cream cones on his head, Sir?

PRINCE: (*To the audience.*) How do they do that? (*To the TWO GUARDS.*) You know, one of those funny hats.

GUARDS: Oh, *that* fool, Sir.

(*The TWO GUARDS go out and the PRINCE hides behind a curtain. The HERALD comes in and plays the imaginary horn.*)

HERALD: Ta da. Ta da. Ta da ... Ta rum tum tum.

PRINCE: (*Coming out from behind the curtain. To the audience.*) Ta rum tum tum? (*He goes back behind the curtain.*)

HERALD: Announcing the court fool.

(*The FOOL enters skipping and throwing confetti in the air. He is wearing a fool's cap and a half mask which covers his eyes and nose. The mask has a long nose.*)

FOOL: (*In a sing-song voice.*) Where are you? Oh, Principoo, where are you? (*He continues dancing around.*) Your fool is here to bring you cheer. (*He makes a face at the audience and forces a laugh.*) Ha ha ha. (*He throws confetti and catches it on his head.*) Rain, rain go away.

(*The PRINCE sticks his foot out from behind the curtain and the FOOL trips and goes sprawling on the floor. The PRINCE roars with laughter and the FOOL has to grudgingly join in as he gets up and dusts himself off.*)

PRINCE: I've got a great idea!

FOOL: (*To the audience.*) That'll be a first.

(*The PRINCE runs to the throne and gets a doctor's reflector which he puts on his head. He also puts on a doctor's stethoscope and a white coat.*)

FOOL: (*To the audience.*) Oh, no. Here we go. (*The PRINCE sits on the throne and pulls a piece of paper out of his pocket. The FOOL pulls out another piece of paper and reads from it.*) Doctor! Doctor! Will that ointment you gave me clear up my spots?

PRINCE: (*Reading.*) I don't make rash promises. (*Laughs.*)

(*After each joke the FOOL dances around throwing confetti and forcing laughter.*)

FOOL:	Doctor! Doctor! I think I'm turning into a goat!
PRINCE:	Stop acting like a kid. (*Laughs.*)
FOOL:	Doctor! Doctor! I just swallowed a roll of film.
PRINCE:	Wait a week and we'll see what develops. (*Laughs.*)
FOOL:	(*To the audience.*) He's a real riot, isn't he. (*To the PRINCE.*) Doctor! Doctor! I've just swallowed a pencil.
PRINCE:	Just sit down and write your name. (*Laughs.*) How am I doing?
FOOL:	Great. A little more practice and you'll have it right. (*To the audience.*) He's getting more *fool*ish by the minute. (*To the PRINCE.*) Doctor! Doctor! I'm turning into a telephone.
PRINCE:	Take two aspirin. If they don't work give me a ring in the morning.
FOOL:	(*To the audience.*) Every great tragedy needs some comedy in it. This is it. (*To the PINCE.*) Doctor! Doctor! I feel terrible. Everyone ignores me.
PRINCE:	Next please!
FOOL:	But I feel like a pack of cards.
PRINCE:	I'll deal with you later.
FOOL:	I feel like a window.
PRINCE:	Where's the pane?
FOOL:	I feel like an apple.
PRINCE:	Come over here. I won't bite you.
FOOL:	But I feel like a sheep.
PRINCE:	That's baaaaaaaad.
FOOL:	(*To the audience.*) And getting worse by the minute. (*To the PRINCE.*) But I'm at death's door.
PRINCE:	Don't worry. I'll pull you through.
	(*The PRINCE laughs heartily and claps the FOOL on the back. The PRINCE freezes and the FOOL approaches the audience and pushes his mask up to his forehead.*)

FOOL: I'll let you in on a secret. I'm not really a fool. In fact, as you can see, I'm the Prince's identical twin — no one can tell us apart. When we were young, no one knew which of us was going to be the Prince of Pomegranate Castle because no one knew which of us was born first. So my evil father sent me off to a distant land where I lived with a peasant family till I learned the truth. Now I have returned disguised as the court fool. All I have to do is get rid of the prince and take his place. No one will ever know the difference.

(*The FOOL pulls his mask back down and steps back in front of the PRINCE. The action begins again.*)

PRINCE: I'm really getting the hang of it, aren't I?

FOOL: Yes, you're a perfect fool.

(*The PRINCE dashes to the throne, takes off the reflector and stethoscope and puts a towel over his arm. He takes another piece of paper out of his pocket.*)

FOOL: (*Aside.*) Oh, no. (*Taking a piece of paper out of his pocket.*) Waiter, waiter! There's a fly in my soup!

PRINCE: (*Reading.*) The rascals don't care what they eat.

FOOL: Waiter, waiter! There's a fly in my soup!

PRINCE: The cook used to be a tailor.

FOOL: Waiter, waiter! There's a fly in my soup.

PRINCE: Don't worry, Sir, the spider in your salad will take care of him.

FOOL: Waiter, waiter! There's a cockroach in my soup!

PRINCE: That's strange, we must have run out of flies.

FOOL: Waiter, waiter! There's a frog in my soup!

PRINCE: He must have eaten the fly.

(*The FOOL freezes and the PRINCE approaches the audience.*)

PRINCE: (*To the audience.*) I suppose you want to know the real reason I called in my fool in the middle of a peasant revolt. Well I'll tell you. I have heard a rumour that this fool, when his mask is off, bears a strong resemblance to His Highness — myself. Now all I have to do is convince him to wear the princely crown when the peasants arrive and it'll be his head and not mine.

(*The PRINCE goes back to the FOOL and the action starts again.*)

FOOL: Waiter, waiter! This soup tastes funny.

PRINCE: Then why don't you laugh?

FOOL: Waiter, waiter! There's something wrong with this soup. I can't eat it. Get the manager.

PRINCE: Save your breath, he won't eat it either.

FOOL: Waiter, waiter —!

PRINCE: Never mind that. I've got an idea. There's a delegation coming to pay tribute to My Highness and I have a great idea for a joke. Let's change places. I'll put on your fool's mask and hat and you can sit on the throne and wear the crown.

| FOOL: | Are you serious? (*To the audience.*) This is going to be easy. |

(*The PRINCE puts the crown on the FOOL's head and puts on the mask. The FOOL picks up the sceptre and sits on the throne and the PRINCE skips around throwing confetti. The HERALD enters holding up the imaginary trumpet.*)

| HERALD: | Ta da. Ta da. Ta rum, ta rum, ta rum. (*To the tune of the William Tell Overture.*) Ta rum, ta rum, ta rum, tum tum. Ta rum, ta rum, ta rum, tum tum. |

| FOOL: | All right! All right! Stop this gag! Who's coming? |

| HERALD: | A delegation of peasants approaches. |

| FOOL: | Where are they? |

| HERALD: | They're just crossing the golden gate bridge. |

| FOOL: | Send them in when they arrive. |

(*The HERALD exits. The PRINCE dances around throwing confetti.*)

| PRINCE: | (*To the audience.*) Now he's in for it. |

| FOOL: | (*To the audience.*) That's what he thinks. |

(*The FOOL hits the PRINCE on the head with his sceptre and knocks him out. He drags him to a chair and sits him in it.*)

| FOOL: | All I have to do is wait for the peasants and listen to their demands and we'll all live happily ever after while my brother starts a new life in a distant land. All I have to do is grant the peasants just what they want. |

| PRINCE: | (*Opening his eyes and talking to the audience.*) Which will be his head. (*He goes unconscious again.*) |

(*The HERALD enters and is about to play the imaginary horn when the PEASANTS rush in and grab the FOOL. The HEADSMAN enters wearing a black hood and carrying a large chopping block and a double-bladed axe.*)

| FOOL: | Wait! Wait! Can't we talk this thing over? |

| PEASANT NO. 1: | It's too late for talk now. |

| FOOL: | Don't be silly, it's only three o'clock. Four o'clock if you're on daylight saving. |

| PEASANT NO. 2: | It's still too late! |

(*The* PEASANTS *drag the* FOOL *to the chopping block. The* HEADSMAN *looks down at him.*)

FOOL: (*To the* HEADSMAN.) Don't I know you!

HEADSMAN: I don't think so.

FOOL: I thought I recognised your hood. What am I saying? Help! Help! I'll grant you anything you wish! I'm the Prince, I can do that!

PEASANT NO. 1: First we want to cut your head off.

FOOL: OK. I mean, *no*! You can't cut off my head. I won't allow it!

PRINCE: (*To the audience.*) The peasants are always trying to get ahead. (*He goes back into his coma.*)

FOOL: (*To the audience.*) That's worse than "the peasants are revolting".

PEASANT NO. 3: Then we'll cut off your hand.

FOOL: (*Aside.*) Things are getting out of hand.

PEASANT NO. 4: And then we'll cut off both your legs.

FOOL: (*Aside.*) I'd take them to court but I wouldn't have a leg to stand on.

(*The PEASANTS hold the FOOL on the chopping block and the HEADSMAN raises his axe in the air. Everyone freezes and the FOOL gets up and comes forward to the audience.*)

FOOL: (*To the audience.*) Do you really think I'm going to let them cut off my head? Never! I have one more card up my sleeve. (*He goes back to the block and puts his head down. Then, just as the PEASANTS come alive again he steps aside and they freeze again. He comes forward to the audience.*) You see, I understand peasants. I know their ways, the way they think, the way they work, the way they play. I know what really makes a peasant tick. (*He goes back to the block and then — again, just as the axe is about to fall — he steps forward again. He looks back at the PEASANTS for a minute and smiles.*) You see, the thing about peasants is that you can always appeal to their sense of decency.

PRINCE: (*He comes out of his coma, speaks and then goes back to sleep again.*) Peasants don't have any decency — that's why they're peasants.

FOOL: Then I'll appeal to their sense of reason.

PRINCE: (*Reviving again.*) They're unreasonable.

FOOL: Then I'll appeal to their sense of honour.

PRINCE: They're dishonourable.

FOOL: Then I'll escape!

(*The FOOL runs for the door.*)

PEASANTS: (*All together.*) Oh, no you won't!

(*The PEASANTS chase him and grab him. They drag him back towards the chopping block.*)

FOOL: You'd better watch it! I know karate, judo, tae-kwon-do and a lot of other foreign words.

PEASANT NO. 5: I have a black belt myself.

FOOL: In karate?

PEASANT NO. 5: No, to hold my pants up.

PRINCE: (*To the audience.*) And they don't have a sense of humour either.

FOOL: Help!

(*They put the FOOL's head on the block and again the HEADSMAN raises his axe.*)

FOOL: Wait! Stop! Hold the show!

HEADSMAN: What do you want? One last cigarette?

FOOL: No, I'm trying to give them up . . . Stop, you're making a big mistake! I'm not Prince Percy of Pomegranate! I'm only a poor fool. The fool is the real Prince.

(*The HEADSMAN lowers his axe and the PEASANTS look over at the PRINCE, still sound asleep.*)

PEASANT NO. 6: What say you?

FOOL: (*To the audience.*) They can't even speak proper English. (*To the PEASANTS*) Unmask him and see if he isn't the true prince.

(*A PEASANT removes the fool's mask from the PRINCE. There is a gasp from all the PEASANTS at once. The PRINCE comes to.*)

FOOL: You see, I am the Prince's twin, cast out of the castle while I was a child and sent to a distant land. Now I'm back to claim my rightful place as Prince of Pomegranate Castle.

PEASANT NO. 7: What's your real name?

FOOL: Pency. Pency, Prince of Pomegranate.

(*The PEASANTS all snicker at his name.*)

FOOL: I can't help my name.

PEASANT NO. 8: All hail Prince Pency!

PEASANTS: (*All together.*) Hail, hail, hail.

(*The FOOL struts to the throne and sits.*)

FOOL: Please don't hail while I'm reigning . . . Now about your demands. I'm prepared to offer you half of your last taxes back.

PEASANT NO. 1: That's not enough!

FOOL: How about three quarters?

PEASANT NO. 2: Still not enough!

PEASANT NO. 3: We want all our taxes back and the money in the treasury too!

FOOL: Well, you can't have it and that's that! I am a royal, not some trifling average person. My parents were princes and theirs

before them. Look at me and you look at centuries of culture and breeding. Some people are meant to be rulers. Some people are meant to be rich. I'm meant to be both. Now get out of here, you peasants, before I have you thrown out.

(*There is a moment of silence and then ...*)

PEASANT NO. 4: Cut off his head!

(*The PEASANTS yell and grab him, placing his head on the block.*)

FOOL: I was only kidding!

PEASANT NO. 5: It's too late now! Let's do it!

PEASANTS: (*All together.*) Do it!

HEADSMAN: Stop! What are we doing! Pency's no better than Percy! Let's chop both their heads off!

PEASANT NO. 9: Two heads are better than one!

(*The PEASANTS grab the PRINCE and the FOOL and put their heads on the block. The HEADSMAN raises his axe. He then stops and while the rest freeze he comes forward and addresses the audience.*)

HEADSMAN: I suppose you're wondering why I told the peasants to cut off both their heads. And I suppose you're also wondering why I wear this hood over my head. (*He takes the hood off.*) As you can see, I'm the spitting image of Percy and Pency. The reason for this is simple: My mother didn't have identical twins, she had identical triplets: Percy, Pency and me. No one could tell us apart so no one knew which one of us was the rightful Prince of Pomegranate Castle. So my evil father sent me off to a distant land where I lived with a peasant family till I learned the truth. And now I have returned to Pomegranate disguised as a headsman. In a second I will be the only monarch around here. (*Raising the axe in one hand.*) All I have to do is eliminate Prince Percy and Prince Pency and the princedom will belong to me: Perky, Prince of Pomegranate.

PEASANTS: (*All together and laughing.*) Perky?!

HEADSMAN: (*To the PEASANTS.*) I can't help my name. (*To the audience.*) So now all I have to do is go back there (*Pointing to the chopping block.*) and do what I've waited years to do.

PEASANTS: Not so fast!

HEADSMAN: What's wrong?

PEASANT NO. 9: What are you going to do for us?

HEADSMAN: I'll give you back all of your last taxes.

PEASANT NO. 10: And the rest of the money in the treasury.

PEASANTS: (*Together.*) Yes!

HEADSMAN: Half of the rest.

PEASANT NO. 11: All of it!

HEADSMAN: Now wait a minute! What am *I* going to live on?

PEASANT NO. 12: We'll give you an allowance of three ducats a week.

HEADSMAN: Three ducats a week?! That's peasants' pay. I can't live on that. You don't understand. (*He struts around the stage with his head in the air.*) I'm no commoner. Through this body surges the blood of kings and queens. I was born to rule. Born to live

in splendour. Born to be rich. I'd rather die than try to live on three ducats a week.

(*There is a moment of silence and then the PEASANTS race towards him screaming. The PRINCE and the FOOL tiptoe towards the door as the PEASANTS grab the HEADSMAN and put his head on the block. PEASANT NO. 1 raises the axe to behead the HEADSMAN.*)

HEADSMAN: I was only joking!

(*Everyone freezes except the PRINCE and the FOOL.*)

PRINCE: (*To the audience.*) They may be revolting but I think these peasants are going to go far.

FOOL: (*To the audience.*) And so are we. (*To the PRINCE.*) Come on, Percy.

(*The PRINCE and the FOOL race out the door, leaving the rest frozen.*)

CURTAIN

CHARACTERS

Trudy
Gerald

NOTE

This skit should be played with the seriousness and intensity of a television soap opera. GERALD wears a long false nose and has a cap pistol in his pocket. These are the only props necessary.

It's a very tricky piece because everything depends on getting the timing right. In general the dialogue should be delivered slowly, leaving time for the characters to pace around the room and to stare meaningfully into each other's eyes the way they do in TV soap operas. But because this is a spoof, everything should be overdone to get the most laughs.

There are some suggestions about how to deliver lines, for example "with feeling" and "soberly" but these are just suggestions. Try it different ways and see what works best. We have put in three dots (. . .) in places where a pause might help get laughs. A dash (—) indicates an interrupted conversation. Whatever you do, don't smile. Keep a straight face.

SCENE

TRUDY TRULOVE is at home alone. She paces back and forth slowly. There is pain on her face. The telephone rings.

THE PLAY

TRUDY: (*Answering the telephone.*) Hello . . . Yes, this is Trudy Trulove . . . (*Excitedly*) Gerald! Yes, darling, I've been hoping you'd ring. It's so good to hear from you, to hear the sound of your voice . . . What? . . . Yes, of course. Oh please, do come over . . . No, darling, it's not inconvenient. It's . . . it's . . . (*With feeling*) convenient . . . Right away, then? OK.

(*Before TRUDY has a chance to put the phone down there is a loud knock at the door. TRUDY opens the door and GERALD is standing there.*)

TRUDY: (*With feeling.*) Gerald.

GERALD: (*With feeling.*) Trudy.

TRUDY: (*With feeling.*) Gerald.

GERALD: (*With feeling.*) Trudy.

TRUDY: Gerald. How long it's been.

GERALD: How very, very long.

TRUDY: How very extremely long.

GERALD: The week has just gone so fast. So very fast.

TRUDY: As fast as a day.

GERALD: Or a minute. (*Snaps his fingers.*)

TRUDY: Or a second, flitting past. (*Snaps her fingers.*)

GERALD: Or an instant.

TRUDY: (*Soberly.*) Is an instant shorter than a second?

GERALD: (*With feeling.*) Yes.

TRUDY: It's been such a long time, Gerald. (*Soberly.*) What do you want?

GERALD: How long have we known each other, Trudy?

TRUDY: Since we were kids running around in bare feet, buying sweets from the corner store, catching frogs in the old swimming hole.

GERALD: A long, long time.

TRUDY: That's true.

GERALD: And how many times have we had romantic dinners together in candle-lit restaurants?

TRUDY: (*With feeling.*) Many times.

GERALD: And how many times have we gone to films . . . to the opera . . . to the ballet . . . and to demolition derbies together?

TRUDY: So many, many times.

GERALD: And how many times have we gone on picnics to the country or gone sailing on my yacht and shared the most intimate secrets of our lives?

TRUDY: A thousand million times, Gerald.

GERALD: And how many times have we flown my plane to a foreign city and then hired a limousine and driven around and around, looking at everything, and then got a flat tyre and had to ring a mechanic only to find that there were none and the car had to be abandoned and we had to hitch-hike in the rain to where we could catch a taxi and then go back to our hotel and get a change of clothes so we wouldn't be late for dinner?

TRUDY: Oh, Gerald. Oh, so many, many countless times.

GERALD: And yet . . .

TRUDY: Yes, Gerald?

GERALD: And yet on all those wonderful romantic occasions — occasions when we told each other the most intimate secrets of our lives — there was always something missing.

TRUDY: Yes, Gerald?

GERALD: Yes, Trudy.

TRUDY: (*Soberly.*) What was missing?

GERALD: I think you know.

TRUDY: I do?

GERALD: There was one thing I never asked you.

TRUDY: (*Soberly.*) That's true.

GERALD: Something . . . something I couldn't ask you.

TRUDY: (*With feeling.*) Oh, why, why, why couldn't you ask me? We have shared our most intimate secrets. You know you could ask me anything. (*Soberly.*) I might say no, but you could ask me just the same.

GERALD: I need some advice.

TRUDY: Advice?

GERALD: Yes, that's when I ask you about something and you give your opinion on it.

TRUDY: I see.

GERALD: You do?

TRUDY: Not yet, I don't.

GERALD: It's about Fran.

TRUDY: Who's Fran?

GERALD: She's just a girl.

TRUDY: Just a girl?

GERALD: A woman. A very special woman. We've known each other since we were children running around in bare feet, buying sweets from the corner store, catching frogs down at the old swimming hole.

TRUDY: She caught frogs with you?

GERALD: Oh, yes, and so many times we had romantic dinners in candle-lit restaurants.

TRUDY: You did?

GERALD: And so many times we went to films . . . to the opera . . . to the ballet . . . and to demolition derbies.

TRUDY: She liked the ballet?

GERALD: Yes. And so many times we went on picnics to the country and sailed on my yacht —

TRUDY: And shared the most intimate secrets of your lives.

GERALD: Then you knew?

TRUDY: (*With rising anger.*) And you flew in your plane to foreign cities and hired a limousine and drove around and around and then had a flat tyre and had to ring for a mechanic only to find that there were none and you had to hitch-hike in the rain to where you could catch a taxi and then go back to your hotel and get a change of clothes so you wouldn't be late for dinner.

GERALD: (*Confused.*) No. That was with you. Don't you remember?

TRUDY: What sort of advice do you want about this, this . . .?

GERALD: Fran.

TRUDY: Yes, Fran.

GERALD: I want to marry her.

TRUDY: (*Quickly.*) Don't.

GERALD: Maybe I'd better explain.

TRUDY: Maybe you'd better.

GERALD: Fran's parents died when she was an infant.

TRUDY:	She was an orphan.
GERALD:	Yes. And she was brought up by her mother's sister.
TRUDY:	Her aunt.
GERALD:	Yes. Then her mother's sister died and so did her mother's sister's husband.
TRUDY:	Her uncle.
GERALD:	Yes. And then he died and she lived for a while with her mother's sister's and her mother's sister's husband's children.
TRUDY:	Her cousins.
GERALD:	Yes. But then her father's mother —
TRUDY:	Her paternal grandmother.
GERALD:	— found out that her son's wife's —
TRUDY:	Fran's son's wife?
GERALD:	No, silly, Fran didn't have a son or a wife. She was only a child.
TRUDY:	So, it was her paternal grandmother's son's wife's —
GERALD:	— sister and sister's husband —
TRUDY:	Fran's aunt and uncle.
GERALD:	— were dead.
TRUDY:	I see. You have such a way with words.
GERALD:	You can't possibly understand. I haven't told you the whole story.
TRUDY:	I'm all ears.
GERALD:	(*Looking at* TRUDY's *ears.*) I've never held it against you. So that's when Fran was locked in a dungeon and made to eat worms.
TRUDY:	(*Angrily.*) She was locked in a dungeon and made to eat worms?
GERALD:	No, I think I'm confusing it with a film I saw. She was sent to a circus where she pretended to be the shortest person in the world because she was so small. Then she grew a lot and pretended to be the tallest person in the world. Finally she grew up and she was normal and she took over the circus and got rich like me.

TRUDY: That rich?

GERALD: Maybe ten dollars less. And she married a man who made glasses.

TRUDY: The drinking sort?

GERALD: No, the seeing sort. He owned a lens-grinding machine. One day when all his workmates were watching, he died.

TRUDY: That's awful. How did it happen?

GERALD: He jumped into it.

TRUDY: You mean —?

GERALD: Yes.

TRUDY: I see . . . he made a spectacle of himself.

GERALD: It was terrible. And it left Trudy all alone in the world. Which brings me to my point.

TRUDY: You want to marry her.

GERALD: You're so perceptive.

TRUDY: Have you ever asked her to marry you?

GERALD: Yes, once I asked for her hand in marriage.

TRUDY: And?

GERALD: She agreed.

TRUDY: She agreed to marry you?

GERALD: Yes, we were engaged. But then she couldn't stand it any longer.

TRUDY: What?

GERALD: My nose.

TRUDY: So she broke if off?

GERALD: No, I wouldn't let her. I was afraid it would hurt too much. But she said she didn't want to marry me. Oh, Trudy, Trudy, Trudy. (*Sobs and grabs* TRUDY, *putting his head on her shoulder.*) What can I do? What can I do? The world is too cruel. I need your advice.

TRUDY: (*Soberly.*) Ask me anything.

GERALD: I was thinking of taking poison.

TRUDY: Don't.

GERALD: Why not?

TRUDY: Shooting's quicker.

GERALD: Yes, of course.

(GERALD *whips out a pistol and shoots himself, all in one quick motion. He falls down.*)

TRUDY: What a tragedy. He asked for her hand but she didn't want his nose. I suppose you couldn't blame her. (*To* GERALD.) Want any more advice?

GERALD: (*Still lying with his eyes closed.*) No thanks.

(TRUDY *steps over* GERALD *and walks off.*)

CURTAIN

This School Is Driving Me Nuts!

A COMEDY MONOLOGUE

NOTE

This piece only needs one actor, a student (you), and no props or costumes. All you have to do is face the audience and speak your lines. If you're not at school, say "*My* school is driving me nuts" instead of "*This* school is driving me nuts." Or say "bonkers" or "crazy" instead of "nuts". But pretend that you're really being driven crazy. Deliver the lines slowly and dramatically and, most of all, never laugh or even smile. Give the audience plenty of time to laugh at the jokes. It might be a good idea to deliver the line "This school is driving me nuts" louder and louder as the piece goes on. Turn your head from left to right in the parts when you're quoting a conversation between a teacher and a student. This will help the audience to know which one is talking. Also practise silly voices when you're quoting.

    You'll probably get more groans than laughs at first because of the very corny humour. Don't worry, just keep going and (hopefully) the audience will start to laugh in spite of themselves.

STUDENT: This school is driving me nuts. I've been to other schools but never one like this. I'll give you an example. On my first day I was late. I'd sprained my ankle. I gave the principal a note but he said it was a lame excuse. (*Pause.*) It's true. Then the music teacher asked me if I was good at picking up music. I said, "Yes," and he said, "Good. Pick up that record player and move it back to my office." (*Pause.*) He gave me a few piano lessons. I thought I was going OK. He even asked me if I'd like to take up the piano as a career. "Sure," I said. "Then why don't you become a piano removalist?" he said. (*Pause.*) That was the day the cookery class burnt something. (*Pause.*) The cookery classroom.

This school is driving me nuts. Seriously, my teacher asked us to name something important that didn't exist fifty years ago and one of the girls in the back yelled out, "Me!" (*Pause.*) It's true. The teacher asked us to write a very long sentence and the same girl came up to the blackboard and wrote two words, "Life imprisonment." "That's the longest sentence you can get," she said. (*Pause.*) We were talking about survival and the teacher asked her to imagine she was an Eskimo walking across the North Pole when she was suddenly attacked by a huge polar bear. "What would you do?" the teacher asked. "I'd throw a spear at him," the girl answered. "What would you do if a second polar bear appeared?" the teacher asked. "I'd throw a spear at him," the girl answered. "And what if a third and a fourth and a fifth bear attacked?" "I'd throw three more spears," the girl answered. The teacher said, "Now wait a minute. Where are you getting all the spears from?" And the girl said, "The same place you're getting all the polar bears." (*Pause.*) It's true. I wouldn't say it if it wasn't true.

(*Loud.*) This school is driving me nuts. One of the kids said to the teacher, (*Making a little boy voice.*) "Teacher? Can I get in trouble for something I didn't do?" And the teacher said, "Don't be silly. Of course not." And the kid said, "Good. I didn't do my homework." (*Pause.*) Later the teacher was giving us a geography lesson and she caught the same boy drawing cartoons in a notebook. She got really angry. (*Angrily.*) "I hope you're learning something," she yelled. "I'm not," the boy said. "I'm listening to you." (*Pause.*) It's true. I swear to you, it's true.

(*Louder*.) This school is driving me nuts. The other day we were having a Maths lesson and the teacher said to a boy in the front row, "If I lend you twenty dollars and ask you to pay me back five dollars every month, how much will you owe me after three months?" The boy thought for a minute and then said, "Twenty dollars." And the teacher said, "I'm afraid you don't know very much about arithmetic." And the boy said, "I'm afraid you don't know very much about me." (*Pause*.) This is all true. The teacher used to blame me for everything. One day she asked us all to write a three-line poem and I wrote a good one. At least I thought it was good. It went like this:

> There was a young man name Ned
> Who wished that he was dead
> So he jumped into a river
>   and the water was over his ankles.

But, no, it wasn't good enough for the teacher. "It doesn't rhyme," she said. (*Angrily*.) Now was it my fault the water wasn't deep enough?

(*Louder still.*) This school is driving me nuts. My teacher was going to tell us all about farm animals. "Pay attention and look at me," she said, "or you'll never learn what a jackass is." (*Pause.*) Honestly, that's what she said. Then she said, "Today we're going to have a discussion on Mount Everest." And one of the girls said, "I can't. I've got to be home by four o'clock." (*Pause.*) "We're not *going* to Mount Everest," the teacher said. "We're going to *discuss* it. You're not very smart, are you?" "I may not be very smart," the girl said, "but I can do something you can't do." "And what might that be?" the teacher asked. "Read my own handwriting," the girl said. (*Pause.*) The teacher got really angry. She looked at the girl and said, "Why is it everything I tell you goes in both ears and out the other?!" (*Pause.*) It's true. That's what she said. She caught one of the kids at the back of the room talking. "Who's doing the teaching here?" she yelled. The kid said, "You are." And the teacher said, "Then why are *you* talking like an idiot?" (*Pause.*) She said, "There's no talking allowed." And the kid said, "How can I talk if I can't talk aloud?"

(*Very loud.*) This school is driving me nuts! Some of the teachers are really strict. One of the boys was sent home because the girl next to him was smoking. (*Angrily.*) Can you imagine that? *He* was sent home because *she* was smoking! (*Pause.*) Of course he's the one who'd set her alight. (*Pause.*) And we have one of the dumbest kids in the world in our class. The other day we had to tell what some words meant. Would you believe he thought blackmail was what you got when the postman dropped your letters down the chimney? (*Pause.*) Would you believe that? He thought that a cartoon is what you sing when you're driving? (*Pause.*) That lawsuits are what solicitors wear? (*Pause.*) That a traffic jam is what cops put on their toast? (*Pause.*) That lemonade is giving money to lemons. (*Pause.*) It's true! That's what he thinks. He thinks that a piano tuner is a musical fish. (*Pause.*) He thinks that apricots are what baby apes sleep on. (*Pause.*) He does. He's so dumb he thinks that Captain Cook is two jobs on a ship. It's all true. I wouldn't lie to you.

(*Yell.*) This school is driving me nuts! It's no wonder no one wants to come here any more. The other day one of the mothers couldn't get her son to go to school. The son said (*Jumping up and down putting on a babyish voice.*) "I don't want to go back to school! I don't want to! I don't want to! Nobody's going to make me go!" And the mother said, "Don't be silly! Act your age! You have to go to school. You're forty-five years old and you're the principal." It's all of it true. Thank you.

(Take a deep bow — you earned it.)

Curtain

53

Muckup at Murder Mansion

CHARACTERS

Detective Inspector McUp
Burglar
Lady Grimsby-Gore
Lady Grimsby-Gore's sister
Lady Grimsby-Gore's brother

STAGING

The play takes place in one room of a mansion but no furniture is needed. If any is used, remember that Grimsby-Gore Mansion is filled with worthless old furniture and paintings. Two entrances are needed. One leads outdoors and the other to the rest of the mansion.

COSTUMES AND PROPS

The GRIMSBY-GORES are very posh and DETECTIVE IN-
SPECTOR McUP wears a detective's suit coat over his black and
white striped jumper. The burglar wears the same type of jumper
as well as a black mask over his eyes. You'll need a cap pistol
to make the sound of a gunshot in the beginning or you can clap
a couple of boards together. Try boards of different lengths till
you get the right sound. Other props you'll need are:

A necklace (*worn by LADY GRIMSBY-GORE*)
A bracelet (*worn by the SISTER*)
A watch (*worn by the BROTHER*)
A magnifying glass
Three pairs of handcuffs

CHARACTERISATION

As with the other plays, don't worry too much about whether
the characters are played by members of the right sex. There's
no reason why a boy can't be made up to play LADY GRIMSBY-
GORE or a girl to play the detective or the burglar. DETECTIVE
INSPECTOR McUP has the most lines to speak but the burglar
has one of the hardest jobs because the actor who plays him has
to lie perfectly still throughout the play.

SCENE

The entrance hall of Grimsby-Gore Mansion. With the curtain
still closed, or the stage black, we hear a gunshot, the thud of
a body hitting the floor and then a blood-chilling scream. The
curtain rises and the BURGLAR wearing a black and white striped
jumper and a black mask around his eyes, lies dead on the floor.
LADY GRIMSBY-GORE bends over him, horrified. There is a
knock at the door and then INSPECTOR McUP enters.

THE PLAY

McUP: Pardon me, Lady Grimsby-Gore, but the door was open. I'm Detective Inspector McUp. (*Pronounced like any Irish name, with the accent on the "Up".*)

GORE: Muckup?

McUP: Not while I'm on duty. I believe there's a bit of a problem here.

GORE: Yes, Inspector. It's only just happened this instant. How did you know?

McUP: We police inspectors have our ways.

(*INSPECTOR McUP goes over to BURGLAR, looks him over very carefully.*)

GORE: What do you think?

McUP: Dead. Not much we can do about it.

GORE: My goodness.

McUP: (*Taking out a notepad and pen.*) All right, confess, Lady Grimsby-Gore. Why did you do it?

GORE: But . . . but . . . I didn't.

McUP: (*To the audience.*) That's what they always say. (*To LADY GRIMSBY-GORE.*) That sort of attitude will get you nowhere. What we like down at the police station is good clean cases; confessions and then full explanations about why the culprits did them. We hate messy, unsolved crimes. You can always plead for mercy and maybe the judge will feel sorry for you.

GORE: But I didn't do anything. I don't even own a gun.

McUP: Ahah! Caught you then!

GORE: What do you mean?

McUP: I didn't mention a gun. I didn't say anything about a murder weapon and yet you know he was shot.

(*INSPECTOR McUP takes out a pair of handcuffs and puts them on LADY GRIMSBY-GORE.*)

McUP: These will keep you from any more funny business.

GORE: But . . . but —

McUP: Did you murder him on purpose or was it an accident?

GORE: Neither.

McUP: There is a difference, Lady Grimsby-Gore. Now if the jury finds you guilty of murdering him by accident you might only get life imprisonment. If you behave yourself in prison — I trust you know how to behave yourself — you could be out roaming the streets again in — say — twenty years —

GORE: But —

McUP: If, on the other hand, you murdered him on purpose, you'll have to go to prison for a whole day.

GORE: Life imprisonment if it was a mistake and only one day if I did it on purpose? That doesn't make sense.

McUP: On the second day they take you out and hang you. Ha ha ha ha ha ha ha! (*He laughs long and loud and then gets hold of himself.*) Sorry, that's just a little joke we have down at the station. Now, are you going to confess or not?

GORE: I didn't do it! I tell you I didn't do it! I heard a scream. I was upstairs in my bedroom watching the late night movie on TV.

McUP: A likely story.

GORE: I think he's a burglar.

McUP: (*Stepping back in surprise.*) A burglar, you say?

GORE: Yes.

McUP: You mean a burglar that breaks into people's houses to steal things?

GORE: Yes, that sort of burglar.

McUP: And what do you suppose he was after?

GORE: I don't know. You see the thing about Grimsby-Gore Mansion is that there's nothing worth taking. All we have are cheap paintings and dreadful moth-eaten furniture.

McUP: You mean there's nothing of value in this mansion?

GORE: Nothing. Burglars break in all the time and they can't find anything to steal. Sometimes they feel so sorry for us they leave a twenty-dollar note on the table. My sister and brother and I never keep anything of value in the house because it might be stolen.

McUP: What's the point of being rich if you can't have things that are worth buckets and buckets of money? You must have *something* valuable. Come on, you can tell me.

GORE: (*Smiling.*) Well, there is one thing.

McUP: What is it?

GORE: My necklace.

(*INSPECTOR McUP quickly studies the necklace with his magnifying glass.*)

McUP: What's it worth?

GORE: A great deal. It was once owned by Queen Sally the Sixth of Saskatchewan.

McUP: Sally of Saskatchewan? How much is it worth?

GORE: I'd rather not say.

McUP: Oh, come on, you can tell me, I'm a police inspector.

GORE: I don't want my sister and brother to know how much it's worth. They'd be jealous. You see, our parents liked me best and they gave it to me. The others only got worthless trinkets.

McUP: How much?

GORE: Promise not to tell?

McUP: (*Holding up three fingers.*) Scouts' honour.

(*LADY GRIMSBY-GORE whispers in INSPECTOR McUP's ear.*)

McUP: (*Shouting.*) A twenty million dollar and fifty cent necklace! Wow! That's a lot of money!

GORE: Shhhhhhh!

(*Lady Grimsby-Gore's SISTER rushes in.*)

SISTER: Is that necklace worth twenty million dollars and fifty cents?

GORE: Yes.

SISTER: But it can't be. It's only a worthless trinket.

GORE: That's a lie! I took it to a jeweller and he said it was worth twenty million dollars and fifty cents. You see, Mummy and Daddy liked me best.

SISTER: No they didn't.

GORE: Yes they did.

(*The SISTER suddenly sees the body on the floor and screams.*)

SISTER: What happened? Who is he? Who killed him?

McUP: Don't pretend you don't know.

SISTER: Who are you?

McUP: Inspector McUp.

SISTER: Muckup?

McUP: Not while I'm on duty. Now, would you like to confess to the murder or will I have to beat it out of you?

SISTER: But I didn't do anything.

McUP: (*To the audience.*) That's what they always say. (*To the SISTER.*) Do you mean to tell me that you didn't kill this poor man?

SISTER: I don't even have a gun.

McUp: Ahah! Who said anything about a gun?

(*INSPECTOR McUp handcuffs the Sister to Lady Grimsby-Gore.*)

Sister: But there's nothing of value in the mansion.

McUp: Nothing?

Sister: (*Smiling.*) Well, not very much.

McUp: You can tell me.

SISTER: Only this bracelet.

(*INSPECTOR McUP examines the bracelet with his magnifying glass.*)

McUP: Where did you get it?

SISTER: My parents gave it to me.

GORE: Mummy and Daddy gave you that?

SISTER: Yes. They liked me best.

GORE: No they didn't!

SISTER: Did so! It's worth more than my sister's silly necklace and my poor old brother only got a worthless trinket.

McUP: How much is it worth?

SISTER: I'm not supposed to tell.

McUP: You can tell me.

SISTER: If I whisper it in your ear, will you promise to keep it a secret?

McUP: Of course I will, I'm a police inspector. Who do you think I am, some big-mouth who tells people's secrets all over town? Police inspectors have to be able to keep secrets or no one would trust them. I mean, if I was a blabbermouth, would anyone ever tell me their secrets? Would they?

SISTER: I suppose not.

McUP: Of course they wouldn't. Now tell me how much it's worth and I won't tell another soul as long as I live. Cross my heart.

(*INSPECTOR McUP crosses his heart and the SISTER whispers in his ear.*)

McUP: (*Shouts.*) A thirty million dollar and forty-two cent bracelet! Wow!

SISTER: Shhhhhhhh!

(*The BROTHER enters.*)

BROTHER: (*To SISTER.*) Is that bracelet that Mummy and Daddy gave you worth thirty million dollars and forty-two cents?

SISTER: Yes.

BROTHER: But I thought it was only a worthless trinket.

SISTER: Well it's not. I had it valued. It was once owned by Queen Tessola the Twelfth of Tasmania.

McUP: Tessie of Tassie?

SISTER: You see, Mummy and Daddy liked me best. (*Sticks her tongue out at LADY GRIMSBY-GORE.*)

GORE and
BROTHER: (*Together.*) They did not!

SISTER: Did so!

(*The BROTHER sees the body on the floor and screams.*)

McUP: (*To the BROTHER.*) I have reason to suspect that you are the murderer. Now, are you going to confess or will we take you down to the police station and beat you with a rubber truncheon until you admit to killing this poor man?

BROTHER: Who are you?

McUP: I'm Inspector McUp.

BROTHER: Muckup?

McUP: Not while I'm only duty. (*To the audience.*) Why do they always ask me that? (*To the BROTHER.*) Now, confess or else!

BROTHER: I didn't do it!

McUP: (*To the audience.*) Do you see? That's what they always say. (*To the BROTHER.*) You'll make things much easier in the long run if you just tell me why you shot him.

BROTHER: Shot him? But I don't even own a gun.

McUP: That does it!

(*INSPECTOR McUP handcuffs the BROTHER to the SISTER.*)

McUP: You gave yourself away. Nobody said anything about a gun.

BROTHER: But you said he was shot.

McUP: I didn't say he was shot by a gun, now did I? He might have been shot by a bow and arrow or an old Roman cross-bow. He could have been shot by a poison-tipped dart from a blowgun shot by a South American Indian. He could have been shot out of a circus cannon. But no, *you* said, 'I don't even own a gun,' and that, smartypants, will send you to the electric chair.

BROTHER: But I don't even know who he was. Why would I shoot a complete stranger?

McUP: He was a burglar who broke in to steal all your valuables and instead of simply ringing the police so I could come and arrest him, you decided to take the law into your own hands and shoot him. You can't just shoot people because you don't approve of what they do for a living. That's for us to do.

BROTHER: But why would I shoot him? There are no valuables in the mansion. Well, only my sister's thirty million dollar and forty-two cent bracelet?

McUP: Nothing else?

BROTHER: Nothing?

McUP: (*Winking at him.*) Not even one teeny weeny valuable thing?

BROTHER: (*Smiling.*) Well . . . maybe one teeny weeny thing.

McUP: What is it?

(*LADY GRIMSBY-GORE and her SISTER lean forward to listen. Their BROTHER shows INSPECTOR McUP his watch.*)

BROTHER: My parents gave it to me. It was worn by King Frank the Forty–Fifth of Frankfurt. It's worth quite a lot of money.

McUP: Frank of Frankfurt? How much?

BROTHER: (*Glancing at his sisters.*) I can't tell.

McUP: You can tell me.

BROTHER: Let's just say it's worth a lot of money.

McUP: Let's just say how much.

BROTHER: Do you promise never to tell anyone, ever?

McUP: (*Giving the Scout salute.*) I promise.

BROTHER: Even if someone punches you and kicks you and offers you a lot of money to tell?

McUP: Nothing will make me tell.

BROTHER: Even if they tie you to railway tracks when a train is coming and refuse to let you go unless you tell?

McUP: I promise I won't tell.

BROTHER: Even if they tickle you?

McUP: I promise. Now tell me how much the watch is worth!

(*The BROTHER whispers in INSPECTOR McUP's ear. INSPECTOR McUP looks at the sisters who are waiting to hear. He paces around the room in silence, thinking about what he's heard.*)

McUP: (*Shouts.*) Fifty million dollars and twelve cents! Wow! That's a lot of money!

BROTHER: You weren't supposed to tell!

McUP: (*Shouts.*) I can't help it! I can't help it! I've never been able to keep a secret (*Nearly in tears.*) I'm sorry, I'm only human and sometimes humans just have to tell secrets!

BROTHER: Then how can you be a police inspector?

McUP: Who said I'm a police inspector?

GORE: You did.

McUP: I did? Oh, yes, I did. That's another thing. I tell lies. Sometimes they're little white lies and sometimes they're fibs and sometimes they're really big, fat, juicy lies. (*Crying.*) I can't help it! I'm only human and sometimes we humans just have to tell lies.

SISTER: But if you're not a police inspector, what are you?

McUP: (*Soberly.*) I thought you'd never ask.

(*INSPECTOR McUP takes off his jacket and underneath is a black and white striped jumper just like the one the burglar is wearing. He puts on a black mask.*)

BROTHER: Why, you're a burglar too!

McUP: Yes, you're right.

(*As INSPECTOR McUP talks, he snatches the BROTHER's watch, the SISTER's bracelet and LADY GRIMSBY-GORE's necklace.*)

McUP: I'm afraid I'm not a goody–goody police inspector who can always keep a secret and who doesn't tell lies and who can resist stealing squillions of dollars worth of jewellery from rich people. (*Yells.*) I'm only human! And humans like to have squillions of dollars, for heaven's sake!

(*INSPECTOR McUP nudges the BURGLAR with his toe.*)

McUP: Time to get up, Frank, I found the goodies.

(*The BURGLAR gets up and dusts himself off.*)

BURGLAR: Next time will you please be a bit quicker? I almost fell asleep.

(*INSPECTOR McUP and the BURGLAR go off.*)

CURTAIN

CHARACTERS

Cleaner & Sound Effects Operator
Producer
Director
Detective
Butler

NOTE

The CLEANER is the central character in this skit and gets all the laughs even though he or she never speaks a line of dialogue. During the whole piece the other actors never notice what the CLEANER is doing. The other actors shouldn't need a lot of rehearsal time to get their parts right but the CLEANER will have to practise doing the sound effects to get as many laughs as possible.

It's a good skit for actors who can't remember their lines because they'll mostly be reading from scripts..

PROPS FOR SOUND EFFECTS

Table (*to knock*)

Wind machine

(*Swinging a thick piece of rope or a stick connected to a rope will make the sound of wind. But* **be careful!** *Or just make the sound of wind with your mouth.*)

Brass bell

Gravel box

(*This could be any box that will fit a couple of inches of coarse gravel. Then put both your feet in to make the sound of someone walking on a gravel path.*)

Dried peas or marbles in a box to make
the sound of rain or hail.

Two small plastic containers

(*Either plastic cups or takeaway food containers will do. Clomp the open ends together to make the sound of horses hooves.*)

A saw and a piece of wood

A plate (*to smash*)

Hammer

Blackboard

SCENE

The DIRECTOR and PRODUCER are talking on stage. A CLEANER walks across the stage behind them, sweeping. The CLEANER stops at the table that has sound effects props on it and looks them over, picking up one or two of the props but without making any noise. The other actors completely ignore the CLEANER throughout the skit.

THE PLAY

PRODUCER: I just found a great new play we could put on. How would you like to direct it?

DIRECTOR: Tell me something about it.

PRODUCER: Here, have a look at this.

(*The PRODUCER hands the DIRECTOR a script. The PRODUCER then waves to two people, the DETECTIVE and the BUTLER, who are offstage. They come on.*)

PRODUCER: Here (*Handing copies of the script to the DETECTIVE and the BUTLER.*) You be the detective and you be the butler. (*To the DIRECTOR.*) Here goes — you're going to love this. (*He puts on a dramatic voice and uses his hands to tell the story.*) The first act starts on a cold and windy night —

(*The CLEANER twirls the wind machine.*)

— when a detective rides up on his horse —

(*The CLEANER makes horses' hoofbeat sounds by hitting the plastic containers together.*)

DETECTIVE: Whoa!

PRODUCER: He gets down from his horse and walks slowly up the gravel path to the old mansion.

(*The CLEANER walks in the gravel box.*)

PRODUCER: And then knocks on the door.

(*The CLEANER knocks on the table.*)

PRODUCER: And then he knocks again.

(*The CLEANER knocks on the table again.*)

PRODUCER: But still no one comes. Inside he can hear the sound of someone sawing wood.

(*The CLEANER saws the piece of wood.*)

PRODUCER: And finally rings the doorbell.

(*The CLEANER rings the brass bell.*)

BUTLER: (*Calling.*) Who is it?

DETECTIVE: It's me, Detective Inspector Brown, from the village. Open the door. I have a few questions to ask.

(*The CLEANER makes a creaking noise with her voice like a large door opening.*)

DETECTIVE: I have here a warrant to search the premises. I received a complaint about mysterious noises. Your neighbours think they're coming from this house.

BUTLER: Search if you must, but I assure you, you'll find nothing amiss in Manor House.

PRODUCER: So the butler closes the door and the detective follows him into the parlour —

(*The* CLEANER *walks on the spot and continues walking.*)

PRODUCER: — and outside it begins to rain —

(*The* CLEANER, *still walking on the spot, makes rain noises by rolling the peas back and forth in the box.*)

PRODUCER: — and the rain suddenly changes to hail —

(*The CLEANER, still walking on the spot, shakes the box violently to make the sound of hail.*)

PRODUCER: — and then back to rain again.

(*The CLEANER, still walking, makes rain noises again.*)

PRODUCER: Suddenly the rain stops.

(*The CLEANER slams the rain box down on the table.*)

PRODUCER: A dog howls in the distance.

(*The CLEANER, still walking, makes a howling noise and then continues howling.*)

DETECTIVE: (*Cupping a hand behind his ear.*) Is that a dog I hear howling in the distance?

BUTLER: Yes, sir, it is a dog howling in the distance.

PRODUCER: Then the howling stops and the detective and the butler stop walking.

(*The CLEANER Stops walking and howling.*)

PRODUCER: They listen and hear the faint sound of tap-dancing in another room.

(*The CLEANER tap-dances lightly.*)

PRODUCER: And the dancing comes closer and closer.

(*The CLEANER's tap-dancing gets louder and louder.*)

DETECTIVE: Is that tap-dancing I hear?

BUTLER: Yes, I believe it is.

DETECTIVE: Just as I thought.

PRODUCER: The tap-dancing gets louder and louder and then there is constant moaning from the mysterious dancer.

(*The CLEANER tap-dances louder and moans at the same time.*)

DETECTIVE: Why it's a ghost! It's dancing all around us now!

PRODUCER: Then it begins to rain again —

(*The CLEANER, still tap-dancing madly and moaning, picks up the rain box and shakes it to make rain noises.*)

PRODUCER: — and then the rain changes to hail.

(*The CLEANER shakes the box violently to make hail noises*.)

PRODUCER: And the dog starts howling in the background again.

(*The CLEANER, still tap-dancing and moaning and shaking the rain box, also howls intermittently. The other actors remain silent as the CLEANER carries on furiously*.)

BUTLER: (*Yells*.) What?!

(*Pause*.)

DETECTIVE: (*Yells*.) I said, it's a ghost!

(*Pause*.)

BUTLER: (*Yells*.) I know!

DETECTIVE: (*Yells*.) You do?!

BUTLER: (*Yells*.) Yes.

(*Pause*.)

PRODUCER: Then the wind picks up again —

(*The CLEANER, now nearly exhausted from tap-dancing, howling, moaning and making the sound of hail, also makes wind noises*.)

PRODUCER: (*In a low voice*.) And in the detective's terror —

DETECTIVE &
BUTLER: (*Together*.) What?!

PRODUCER: (*In a loud voice*.) In the detective's terror, he knocks over a statue which smashes to the ground.

(*The CLEANER smashes a plate on the floor*.)

PRODUCER: And then everything is deathly quiet.

(*The CLEANER stops making sound effects and collapses on the table*.)

BUTLER: You've done it! You've broken the curse of Manor House!

DETECTIVE: Who was that ghost?

BUTLER: That was the ghost of the fourth Duke of Cornwall and York. He was doomed to tap-dance for all eternity because he killed a band leader. But you smashed his statue and that must have broken the curse.

DETECTIVE: Tell me one last thing before I go. Why was he moaning?

BUTLER: I thought that was obvious. His shoes were too tight.

(*The CAST laughs except for the CLEANER who gives them a dirty look.*)

PRODUCER: Well, did you understand it?

DIRECTOR: Sure. It was clear as a bell —

(*The CLEANER rings the bell.*)

DIRECTOR: — but we'll have to get the selection committee's stamp of approval.

(*The CLEANER stamps her foot.*)

PRODUCER: I'm sure it could be a real pop hit —

(*The CLEANER makes a popping noise with her mouth and then hits the table with her fist.*)

PRODUCER: — a real scream —

(*The CLEANER screams.*)

PRODUCER: — if they can scrape together the money.

(*The CLEANER slowly scratches the blackboard.*)

PRODUCER: I've got to go now. I've got to buy three pounds of sausages for the cast barbecue.

(*The CLEANER pounds the table with a hammer three times.*)

PRODUCER: But there could be a problem.

DIRECTOR: Like what?

PRODUCER: Who can we get to do the sound effects?

CURTAIN

Waiting
for
Joe Doe

CHARACTERS

Bugsey
Bombshell Betty
Mugs
Mona
Joe Doe
Trio Jack
Bodyguard No. 1
Bodyguard No. 2
Bodyguard No. 3
Weasel Willy
Baby Calhoun
Nanny
Blind Billy
Happy Harry

STAGING

The action all takes place in one room, an office in an old building in Chicago in the 1930s. There are doors at each side of the stage and there is one window. The office could be a grotty, single-desk office that hasn't been used for some time, with chairs lying on their sides.

COSTUMES AND PROPS

Very few props and costumes are needed. The actors could be dressed in mock 1930s gangster clothes, the men in pin-stripes and/or trench coats and wearing hats. BOMBSHELL BETTY is dressed as a typical floozie with a tight dress split up the side and a wide hat and gloves. MONA is in similar clothes but looks more the dolly-bird secretary. NANNY is dressed as a typical English nanny. BABY CALHOUN should be wearing a baby's white skull-cap and perhaps even have a dummy in his mouth when first seen.

BUGSEY, MUGS and JOE DOE each have pistols.

There are six machine guns between TRIO JACK and the three BODYGUARDS, WEASEL WILLY and BABY CALHOUN.

BLIND BILLY needs a white cane and dark glasses.

The play calls for a cap pistol or other means of making the sound of gunshots.

A pram large enough for BABY CALHOUN is needed.

CHARACTERISATION

Of the fourteen characters, eleven are nominally male. The roles of MONA, BOMBSHELL BETTY and NANNY could be played either by girls or boys dressed as women, and similarly, the gangsters can be boys or girls dressed as men.

BUGSEY is a simpleton and MUGS is even more so.

BOMBSHELL BETTY and MONA are quick-witted but rough.

JOE DOE is tough and quick in his movements as is WEASEL who, as his name implies, is shifty as well.

TRIO JACK is as thick as a brick, maybe even dumber than BUGSEY and MUGS.

The three BODYGUARDS are typical heavies. They're a bit dull but more quick-witted than TRIO JACK.

HAPPY HARRY is a typical gangster boss, tougher and smarter than his men.

BLIND BILLY is deadpan. We can't tell what he's like because of the dark glasses.

SCENE

The scene is an empty office on the South Side of Chicago in the 1930s. BUGSEY, a small-time gangster, comes in. He looks at his watch and paces for a minute and then starts combing his hair in his reflection in the window. BOMBSHELL BETTY comes through the door.

THE PLAY

BUGSEY: (*Self-consciously looking at himself in the glass.*) Hello Betty. How's tricks? (*Pause.*) Do you think I'll lose my looks when I get older?

BETTY: I certainly hope so. (*Laughs.*) Say, did you know that the smartest woman in Chicago is going deaf?

BUGSEY: You don't say ... who's that?

BETTY: (*Cupping a hand behind her ear.*) Eh? (*Pause.*) Eh? (*Laughs.*) Get it?

BUGSEY: (*Laughing weakly.*) Oh, yeah. That's good. That's a rich one.

BETTY: That's Happy Harry's joke. He's got a million of them. (*Severely.*) But Harry's not too happy right now.

(*BOMBSHELL BETTY takes an envelope out of her handbag and hands it to BUGSEY. BUGSEY opens it and removes a wad of money and a note. He glances at the note, moving his mouth as he reads it.*)

BUGSEY: Yeah?

BETTY: Yeah. In particular he is not happy with one Joe Doe, which is the reason you are here.

BUGSEY: (*Still looking at the note, he gives a long, low whistle.*) What'd Joe do to Harry?

BETTY: Dunno. Guess he got under his skin.

(*BETTY turns to go.*)

BUGSEY: (*Counting the money.*) Wait! There's only ten c-notes here.

BETTY: A thousand bucks, that's right.

BUGSEY: It's not enough. I've got a partner. Besides, there are guys on the East Side who get two grand.

BETTY: Harry said the price is a thousand bucks so it's a thousand bucks. Take it or leave it. Don't you know there's a depression going on?

BUGSEY: I'm gonna take this up with Harry.

BETTY: You already did and where did it get you? A thousand bucks is the price if you work alone or with a partner. Bye, now.

(*BOMBSHELL BETTY leaves. In a minute MUGS comes in.*)

MUGS: (*To BUGSEY.*) What's wrong, Bugsey?

BUGSEY: Nuthin' and everything.

MUGS: (*Sniffing the air.*) Is that perfume I smell?

BUGSEY: It is and you do. (*MUGS sniffs his armpits.*) You look terrible. What's the matter with you?

MUGS: I don't feel too good.

BUGSEY: Take some aspirin.

MUGS: I can't, it gives me a headache. (*Pause.*) So what's up?

BUGSEY: We're gonna rub out Joe Doe.

MUGS: (*Giving a long, low whistle.*) Kill Joe Doe? That's pretty rough, isn't it?

BUGSEY: (*Handing five banknotes to MUGS.*) It doesn't get much rougher. Here.

MUGS: But that's only five c's.

BUGSEY: That's what Happy Harry's paying.

MUGS: There ought to be a law. (*Pause.*) Where do we do it?

BUGSEY: Right here. Joe Doe thinks he's on an errand for the boss. When he walks through that door he won't be expecting anything and (*Pointing his fingers like pistols.*) adios.

MUGS: Adios?

BUGSEY: It means goodbye in Spanish.

MUGS: Oh. (*Pause.*) It's a good thing I wasn't born in Spain.

BUGSEY: Why?

MUGS: I don't speak a word of Spanish.

(*BUGSEY and MUGS pull their pistols out of their shoulder holsters and check them. BUGSEY puts his away and MUGS plays with his, twirling it around his finger.*)

BUGSEY: Hey! Did you hear that the smartest woman in Chicago is going deaf?

MUGS: Oh yeah? Who's that?

(*BUGSEY cups a hand behind his ear and suddenly realises that there's something wrong with the joke.*)

BUGSEY: Forget it.

MUGS: Who is she?

BUGSEY: Never mind. Bombshell Betty.

MUGS: The Bombshell is the smartest woman in Chicago? How do you like that? (*Pause.*) Hey, what about this money?

BUGSEY: Don't you know there's a depression going on? Take it up with Harry.

MUGS: I did.

BUGSEY: What'd he say?

MUGS: He just smiled. That's all Happy Harry ever does. He's a cheapskate, that's all.

BUGSEY: And we're today's bargain. Things will be different when we all get together.

MUGS: Yeah. When we get the union started things will be different.

BUGSEY: We'll bring this town to a stop if we don't get a fair deal.

MUGS: Then we'll be calling the shots. No more long hours. No more work on Sunday.

BUGSEY: And no more massacres to save money. One at a time or nothing.

MUGS: Yeah. (*Pause.*) I passed your house last night.

BUGSEY: Thanks. (*Pause.*) Where were you going?

MUGS: I went to a movie with Tricksie.

BUGSEY: Did it have a happy ending?

MUGS: Yeah, I was glad when it was over.

(*There's a knock at the door, MUGS and BUGSEY pull out their pistols.*)

BUGSEY: (*In a low voice to MUGS.*) Shhhhhh. It's him. (*To the person at the door. Singing the line.*) Come in.

(*MONA comes into the room and MUGS and BUGSEY stare at her in disbelief.*)

MUGS: (*To BUGSEY.*) That's not him.

MONA: (*Pushing their pistols down with her hands.*) No kidding. I'm Mona, Happy Harry sent me.

MUGS: Where's Joe Doe?

MONA: Never mind that. Joe squared things with the boss.

BUGSEY: Joe Doe made up with Happy Harry?

MONA: That's what I said, didn't I? He's OK now.

MUGS: Then we're not going to bump him off?

MONA: Of course not. But the good news is you've got a new target: Trio Jack. He'll be here in a few minutes.

MUGS: Trio Jack? What'd he do?

MONA: Let's just say that he got on the boss's nerves. Oh, one more thing. The boss wants two hundred back.

(*MONA holds out her hand for the money.*)

MUGS: What for? The contract's for a grand.

MONA: That was the contract on Joe Doe. The contract on Trio Jack is only eight bills.

BUGSEY: Why only eight?

MONA: Simple. Joe Doe is a very dangerous man. He is one of the sharpest hoods in the city. He can smell a trap like a fox smells chickens. Do you think he would have walked through that door and just let you plug him?

MUGS: Wouldn't he?

MONA: He would not. Joe's as fast as a deer. That's why they call him Joe Doe. He wouldn't have knocked. He'd have dived through that door with his gun blazing. You'd have earned your grand. Now give me the money back.

(*MUGS and BUGSEY are obviously rattled by what MONA has said. They look at each other for a moment and then put their guns away and each take out a hundred-dollar note. MONA snatches the money and turns to go.*)

MUGS: Wait a minute. What's this Trio Jack guy like?

MONA: He's a pushover. Jack is thick as a brick. He doesn't have the brains to tie his shoelaces. No sweat. (*Laughs.*) Hey, have you heard Harry's latest?

BUGSEY: Latest what?

MONA: Latest riddle, dummy.

(*BUGSEY pushes MUGS out of the way.*)

BUGSEY: Tell me.

MONA: (*In a stage whisper to BUGSEY.*) Spell two words that have over a hundred letters.

BUGSEY: Beats me.

MONA: (*Spelling.*) P-O-S-T O-F-F-I-C-E. (*Laughs.*) Isn't that great? Harry's such a funny guy.

(*BUGSEY is still baffled and MONA exits laughing. Finally, BUGSEY laughs lightly as if he's got the joke.*)

MUGS: What was it, Bugsey?

BUGSEY: OK, listen carefully. Spell a post office that has over a hundred letters in it.

MUGS: I don't get it.

BUGSEY: You don't get anything. You can't even spell.

MUGS: I once got an A in spelling.

BUGSEY: There is no A in spelling, you fool.

MUGS: It was a spelling bee.

BUGSEY: Don't be silly. Anyone can spell B.

(*MUGS tries to twirl his pistol again but drops it and then picks it up again.*)

BUGSEY: We had a very close call. It's a good thing Joe Doe didn't come in with guns blazing.

MUGS: Yeah. But what about the money? I coulda used the extra c-note.

BUGSEY: Yeah, me too. But it's worth it not to have to go up against Joe Doe.

(Suddenly the door flies open and JOE DOE dives in, pistol in hand, rolls on the floor and points it at BUGSEY and MUGS. BUGSEY doesn't have time to draw and MUGS drops his pistol accidentally as the door opens.)

JOE: Bang! Bang! *(Laughs.)* Are you Bugsey and Mugs?

BUGSEY & MUGS: *(Together.)* Yeah.

JOE: I'm Joe Doe. Happy Harry sent me to tell you that the contract on Trio Jack is off.

MUGS: It's off?

JOE: Yeah, that's the word. Jack's made things right with the boss. But don't worry. Happy Harry wants you to take care of Weasel Willy instead.

BUGSEY: Weasel Willy? What'd he do?

JOE: I don't know. He musta rubbed Harry the wrong way.

MUGS: Does this mean we get to keep the dough?

JOE: Sure . . . most of it. Harry wants two hundred back.

(JOE holds out his hand.)

BUGSEY: Now wait a minute. The contract was for eight c's.

JOE: That was the contract on Trio Jack. The contract on the Weasel is for six. Count your blessings, boys. Trio Jack is a dangerous man. He never travels without his three bodyguards. That's why they call him Trio. You mighta got Jack but you'da had your work cut out for you with his heavies.

(MUGS and BUGSEY stare at each other in disbelief. Together they reach in their pockets and pull out a hundred dollars each. JOE takes the money and starts to go.)

BUGSEY: Hey, wait a minute! What's this Weasel Willy like?

JOE: Total creep. Nothing to worry about. He's afraid of his own shadow. If you can't handle the Weasel there's something wrong with you. (*Laughs.*)

BUGSEY: What's so funny?

JOE: That Happy Harry is a funny guy.

BUGSEY: (*Waving MUGS away.*) Tell me.

JOE: (*To BUGSEY in a stage whisper.*) What do you give a dame who has everything? (*Pause.*) My phone number.

(JOE DOE exits laughing.)

MUGS: Yeah?

BUGSEY: What do you give a dame who has everything?

MUGS: Beats me.

BUGSEY: (*Laughing.*) Joe Doe's telephone number.

MUGS: (*Puzzled.*) Why?

BUGSEY: I don't know. It's just a joke.

MUGS: Not a very funny one. I liked the post office one better.

(*MUGS throws his pistol in the air and catches it.*)

BUGSEY: Another close one, eh?

MUGS: Yeah and two hundred less.

BUGSEY: I don't like it either. Don't worry about it.

MUGS: Well of course I'm going to worry about it. That's six hundred — three hundred each — to hit Willy the Weasel. That's peanuts. That's nothing. It'll hardly pay for the lead. I gotta house that's falling down. Sometimes I think the only thing that's keeping it up are the termites holding hands.

BUGSEY: Stop griping. There's a depression going on and beggars can't be choosers. Besides, all we have to do is exercise our trigger fingers. It woulda been different if it was Joe Doe or Trio Jack, but Weasel Willy?

MUGS: I still don't like it.

(*MUGS throws his pistol in the air again and drops it. Suddenly the door flies open and TRIO JACK and his THREE*

BODYGUARDS *come in with machine guns in hand. TRIO JACK'S shoelaces are untied. MUGS is bent over, about to pick up his pistol and BUGSEY doesn't have time to pull his pistol out of its shoulder holster.*)

JACK: (*Very slow and dopey.*) Hello boys. Nothing to worry about, it's just Trio Jack. Happy Harry sent me to tell you —

BUGSEY: Not to shoot the Weasel.

(*TRIO JACK opens his mouth to speak but he's too slow. BODYGUARD NO. 1 answers for him.*)

BODYGUARD NO. 1: That's right, that's right, you're a smart boy. It's off.

MUGS: (*To TRIO JACK.*) Why's it off?

(*Again TRIO JACK is too slow in answering.*)

BODYGUARD NO. 2: They kissed and made up. Harry and the Weasel are like that now. (*He holds up crossed fingers.*)

BUGSEY: (*To* TRIO JACK.) So that's the bad news, is there any good news?

BODYGUARD NO. 3: The good news is that Harry's got another job for you.

MUGS: Yeah? Who is it now?

(*TRIO JACK looks around to see if he's going to be permitted to answer. The BODYGUARDS defer to him.*)

JACK: (*Slowly.*) Baby Calhoun.

(*BUGSEY and MUGS put their hands over their money pockets when they hear the name.*)

BUGSEY: Baby Calhoun? Who's that?

BODYGUARD NO. 1: He's just a kid but he gives Harry the pip, that's all. Now there's one thing Harry wanted us to discuss about this contract on Baby Calhoun.

MUGS AND BUGSEY: Oh, no you don't!

BODYGUARD NO. 2: Gentlemen, gentlemen, please. The Baby is no problem. Four hundred is all he's worth. Not like the Weasel. If you'd have gone for the Weasel, you'd have given yourself some real problems. That guy is so cunning you wouldn't have had a chance.

BUGSEY: What do you mean?

BODYGUARD NO. 3: What do you mean, what do we mean? He wouldn't have just come in that door. He'd have been up the fire escape and through that window behind you. You wouldn't have known what hit you.

(*BUGSEY and MUGS take out a hundred dollars each and hand it to JACK. Suddenly the BODYGUARDS start tittering. TRIO JACK is puzzled at first and then laughs out loud. BUGSEY comes up close and MUGS walks away obediently. TRIO JACK and the BODYGUARDS huddle around BUGSEY and speak in rapid succession.*)

JACK: A fella goes to a psychiatrist — right?

BUGSEY: Yeah?

BODYGUARD NO. 1: And the psychiatrist says, "You're crazy."

BODYGUARD NO. 2: And the fella says, "I want a second opinion."

BODYGUARD NO. 3: And the psychiatrist says, "You're ugly, too."

(*TRIO JACK and the BODYGUARDS exit laughing. BUGSEY, smiling, waves MUGS over.*)

BUGSEY: This fella goes to an ugly psychiatrist.

MUGS: An ugly psychiatrist?

BUGSEY: Yeah. Don't interrupt.

MUGS: Aren't they all ugly?

BUGSEY: Of course they're not. Now listen. A fella goes to this ugly psychiatrist and gets a second opinion.

MUGS: Is that it?

BUGSEY: Yeah, that's it. He's crazy, you see? Now pick up that pistol before Baby Calhoun gets here.

MUGS: (*Musing.*) So Betty's going deaf.

BUGSEY: Yeah.

(*MUGS picks up his pistol and puts it in his shoulder holster.*)

MUGS: Up the fire escape, eh?

(*BUGSEY and MUGS both turn towards the window. Just then WEASEL WILLY sneaks in through the door and points a machine gun at them.*)

WEASEL: Reach!

(*BUGSEY and MUGS raise their hands. They turn around slowly.*)

BUGSEY: Weasel Willy?

WEASEL: Yeah.

(*WEASEL WILLY grins and puts his gun away.*)

BUGSEY: You do know how to scare a guy.

WEASEL: It's OK. I just came to say that Baby Calhoun's not the mark. The boss is back in with the Baby. But Harry says that the dude that particularly annoys him at this moment is Blind Billy who, as it happens, will be coming along soon.

MUGS: Blind Billy?

(*BUGSEY and MUGS reach into their pockets and pull out a hundred dollars each. They hand the money to WEASEL WILLY.*)

WEASEL: Thanks. You won't regret this. Baby Calhoun is one of the most dangerous —

BUGSEY: OK, OK. What's Billy like?

WEASEL: No sweat. Blind in one eye and can't see out of the other. Walks with a white cane. Never seen the light of day. If that isn't the easiest two bills you ever earned, I don't know what is. Not like Baby Calhoun.

MUGS: (*Yells*) I don't want to hear how dangerous Baby Calhoun is!

WEASEL: All right, all right. Keep your shirt on.

(*WEASEL WILLY smirks and then signals to BUGSEY to come close. MUGS puts his fingers in his ears.*)

WEASEL: A fella is just getting out of the loony bin and his wife says, "How do you feel?" "Terrible," he says, "But why?" she says. "You're all better now." "How would you feel," he says, "if one day you were Napoleon and the next day you were nobody?"

(*WEASEL WILLY laughs. BUGSEY is puzzled. He turns to MUGS and then WEASEL WILLY looks around furtively and scurries out the door before BUGSEY and MUGS know what's happened.*)

MUGS: Well?

BUGSEY: Well what?

MUGS: Happy Harry's joke.

BUGSEY: Forget it.

MUGS: (*Yelling.*) I want to hear it!

BUGSEY: OK, OK. Don't get your dander up. Napoleon is just getting out of a loony bin and his wife asks how he feels. "Terrible," he says. "But you're OK now," she says. "Yeah," he says, "but how would you feel if you were nobody one day and Napoleon the next?"

MUGS: (*Laughs after a long pause.*) That's good. I like that. (*Soberly.*) Two hundred bucks, eh?

BUGSEY: Yeah.

MUGS: Don't ever tell anyone about this, will ya?

BUGSEY: Don't worry.

(*There's a knock at the door and* BUGSEY *and* MUGS *draw their pistols.*)

BUGSEY: Is that him?

(*They hear a woman's voice outside.*)

NANNY: You-hoo! Anyone there?

MUGS: This place is like Grand Central Station.

(*MUGS and BUGSEY put their pistols away.*)

BUGSEY: (*Sings.*) Come in.

(*NANNY, dressed in a uniform, comes in pushing a pram.*)

MUGS: Listen, lady, I think you're in the wrong place. This is not the Mother Goose Nursery.

(*BABY CALHOUN sits up suddenly in the pram and levels a machine gun at BUGSEY and MUGS.*)

BABY: That's what you think.

BUGSEY: (*Angrily.*) If you're Baby Calhoun and you came to tell us not to rub out Blind Billy then forget it! Forget the whole thing because we're going to do the job and we don't care what you or Joe Doe or Trio Jack or Weasel Willy or even Happy Harry say about it. We're going to rub out Blind Billy and keep the two hundred and that's that! Now get out of here!

(*BABY CALHOUN stares at them in disbelief for a minute and then he and NANNY start to laugh to themselves.*)

BUGSEY: And we don't want to hear any more of Happy Harry's jokes. They're just not funny!

(*BUGSEY grabs BABY CALHOUN'S machine gun and points it at BABY and NANNY.*)

BUGSEY: All right, now. Into the other room, you two, and no funny business.

(*NANNY wheels the pram through the door on the other side of the stage.*)

MUGS: What'd you do that for?

BUGSEY: We've got to make a stand somewhere.

MUGS: But what will Harry say?

BUGSEY: Nothing. We hit Blind Billy and then we take Baby and Nanny for a ride. He'll never know what happened to them.

MUGS: Yeah, good idea.

(*Suddenly they hear the sound of a cane tapping outside. It gets closer and closer.*)

MUGS: It's him!

BUGSEY: Yeah. It's Blind Billy all right. Get ready.

(*They pull out their pistols again and wait as the tapping gets closer and closer. Finally the door opens slowly and BLIND BILLY taps his way into the room. He's wearing black glasses. BUGSEY looks at him tentatively and then steps forward and waves a hand in front of BLIND BILLY's eyes.*)

BUGSEY: (*Laughs.*) It's him all right!

(*MUGS advances and then puts his fingers in his mouth and makes a ridiculous face at BLIND BILLY. He steps back and laughs. BUGSEY laughs and does a little dance in front of BLIND BILLY. He does a spin with one finger on his own head. MUGS howls with laughter. The two of them clown around and scream with laughter. MUGS doubles over in convulsions of laughter and BUGSEY falls on the floor and rolls around. Gradually the laughter dies down. BLIND BILLY puts out his hand as if feeling in BUGSEY's direction. He then does the same in MUGS' direction. He points his white cane at MUGS and there is a blast and MUGS falls dead. He then points it at BUGSEY and shoots him too.*)

BLIND BILLY: (*Calling to off.*) It's OK, Harry, I think I got 'em.

(*HAPPY HARRY enters. He is not smiling.*)

HARRY: Good work, Billy.

(*HAPPY HARRY reaches into MUGS and BUGSEY's pockets and pulls out the remaining two hundred dollar notes. He hands one to BILLY.*)

HARRY: (*To BLIND BILLY.*) Thanks. (*Calling to off.*) Come on, you mugs.

(*BOMBSHELL BETTY, MONA, JOE DOE, TRIO JACK and his three BODYGUARDS, and WEASEL WILLY come in. HAPPY HARRY pulls out a wad of hundred dollar notes and hands one to each of them. NANNY wheels BABY CALHOUN's pram in from the other direction. HAPPY HARRY hands the last hundred dollar bill to BABY CALHOUN but NANNY snatches it away from him.*)

HARRY: There. Two for the price of one. A real bargain. Now, does anybody else think they deserve a raise?

ALL: No boss.

HARRY: (*Smiling.*) You make Harry a very happy man.

CURTAIN